MARY MAGDA...

REVELATIONS FROM A

FIRST CENTURY AVATAR

Volume I

Gloria Amendola

Mary Magdalene:
Revelations from a First Century Avatar
Volume I
(Second Edition)
Gloria Amendola

http://www.gloria-amendola.com/
© 2013, 2020 Gloria Amendola

ISBN: 978-1-944066-27-7

In Publication Data
Amendola, Gloria
Categories:
1.Mind, Body, and Spirit 2. Channeling & Mediumship
BISAC Code: OCC003000

Table of Contents

Introduction

As we continue to redefine Mary Magdalene at this time, we are painting a much fuller picture of this most enigmatic woman of the first century. Piece by piece we are figuring out the true identity of this alleged sinner-saint of the Christian Bible's New Testament.

After thirteen years of study and travel to understand her legacy more fully, there's one thing I'm certain of – who we've been told Mary was, is, quite simply, wrong. I have come to learn that she was so much more than I ever thought she could be, she who arose in the shadow of the great teacher and healer named Jesus.

We owe it to ourselves to keep going until we get her story straight, for when we get her story right, other stories will make more sense. And when that happens, the fog in our minds that's been swirling about for hundreds of years, dare I say thousands, will begin to lift.

We owe it to future generations to take this journey, to reestablish our true spiritual legacy. And that must include the feminine alongside the masculine. In order to foster love and respect between male and female, we must learn how we got from where we were, to where we are now. Both sexes need to learn a more accurate history that reflects what happened through the ages.

And that includes the fact that the Vatican has controlled world populations for centuries via the establishment of a religion that has kept people in the dark, perpetually worshipping a suffering god. It's time to move from the crucifixion to the understanding that the life of Jesus and Mary Magdalene – and their inner circle of disciples – was about undergoing initiations to prepare themselves to learn and directly experience the Mysteries. Their lives were examples of courage and of doing the inner work of self-transformation so they could show people the fullness of life.

As far as I'm concerned, until the Vatican either accepts women as their spiritual equals, or falls from their coveted seat of power, there will never be gender balance in our world.

They know the true story of Jesus. However, they've continued to bury it deep in the Vatican archives. But soon there will be no place for them to hide. Full disclosure of Mary Magdalene is inevitable. They know it, as they understand the ramifications of this new cycle of time. It's their business to know these things! And since the Vatican is so strongly tied to the lie of the Mary Magdalene story, and of the Jesus story for that matter, I must continue to bring up its name and remind people that it's not okay to allow the misinformation campaign to continue on to this day.

If they could just bring themselves to disclose what they know about her beyond the 1969 papal bull, maybe that disclosure could become a healing balm for their broken church. But they must reconcile their deep-seated beliefs about the sacred feminine in order to embrace the goddess.

In the meantime, we owe it to everyone alive today, and especially for the guardians of the grail of the past, to seek out the truth of our spiritual legacy, a legacy left behind by great teachers and healers that heralded from even before the Jesus era. But let me be clear – this legacy is not about religion. This is about spirituality, and it doesn't require a church or interceding priesthood.

This legacy is about our biological and physiological sustainability, and the sustainability of land, sea, and air. And it's not a luxury at this time. It's becoming an absolute necessity!

As you read through this little book, don't let its size fool you. There are veiled esoteric teachings that are seeping out through these pages. There are rich and complex life stories offered for your consideration. Magdalene has revealed interesting fragments of her early life, and of her meeting Jesus again, once her own training was finished. She offers riveting accounts of her life and time with her beloved, but in a way you may not have read before. Some of the details are startling and yet, in some strange way, they feel right to me.

⚜ ⚜ ⚜

Some of the accounts given to me by channeling Magdalene are things I've not heard until now. Mary says it's a new era and after thousands of years, it's time to reveal this information. Did she say thousands of years? Yes, yes she did!

Mary says she and Jesus, or Yeshua as he will also be called throughout this book, feel we are ready to receive these most potent teachings, the teachings of their once-secretive inner circle.

So take a deep breath. Feel the Magdalene enter into the room, her flowing burgundy cloak covering her long auburn hair. As she removes her mantle, she begins to reveal herself to you. And as you read her words, listen closely, for this is the voice of a master.

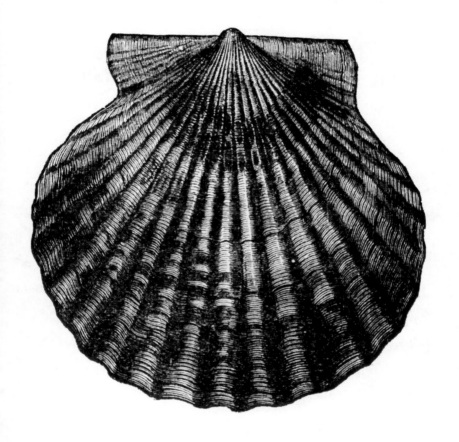

AN UNEXPECTED
PILGRIMAGE

Chapter 1

An Unexpected Pilgrimage:
My Journey with Mary Magdalene

By the time I turned twenty, I had already moved away from the Catholic Church and began learning about other Christian faiths. Throughout the years I attended church services that were Episcopalian, Baptist, Lutheran, Evangelical, and Pentecostal. There were probably others, but those are the ones I can remember. I just had this burning desire to learn a more complete Jesus story; but no matter how much I searched, only bits and pieces made sense. No matter what I read or studied, or what sermons I heard, something was always missing.

It was Easter season in the year 2000. I had decided to go to Sunday service with family and friends. I'd been to this church before and was familiar with their beliefs, although not in agreement with them. The one thing I did enjoy about this church though was its music ministry. It was spirited and lively and could be deeply moving. Yes, there I was again, in church and in conflict.

When the music and the singing ended, the sermon was soon to follow. The charismatic preacher was about to begin his homily He was a powerful speaker and very articulate.

The pastor stood up and told his congregation that he was only going to focus on Jesus. Jesus, Jesus, Jesus. He said he wouldn't discuss Mother Mary at all – just Jesus. Then he continued on, as if his assertion was somehow okay. Well it wasn't okay by me!

It was his declaration of denial of the feminine that was my tipping point. How dare he say he wouldn't even acknowledge Mother Mary! Underneath his bold pronouncement, underneath that denial of her presence and her power, I knew he was denying the feminine. I knew there were men in positions of authority in his church, people he appointed, who were proclaiming policies that did not support women. At all. And that angered me. No wonder why I was conflicted!

I came home that day from church and decided right then and there I was going to write a play about a woman in the bible. That was it. It was time to tell their forgotten stories. I was going to give them a voice. So that week I went to the local library and checked out a bunch of books on women from both the Old and New Testaments of the Bible.

One night after work I sat down at my dining room table with a cup of coffee and the two piles of books that lay there, waiting. It was time to summon the energy to review them.

I opened one of the books on Mary Magdalene and it was as if a life force jumped out of the book and formed a hologram that appeared before me. The image was that of Mary Magdalene; she was jumping up and down and yelling out – "pick me, pick me!"

I was startled. It was as if she were alive, calling out to me to choose her story!

Chills ran up and down my spine. In that moment I had no clue what lay before me but it felt pretty big. As surprising as this may sound, my understanding of Magdalene in the year 2000 was that she was the prostitute Jesus saved from sin. That's what was taught to me in my Catholic education and I never dug deeper. My family focused on Mother Mary and other Catholic saints, but never on Saint Mary Magdalene. I don't recall her name ever being mentioned when I was growing up. It was as if she didn't exist.

Who knew the amount of information I found on Mary Magdalene would be so overwhelming! How would I ever make sense of it all? The pilgrimages in Europe in her name, the cathedrals throughout the world built in her honor, the Knights Templar protecting her legacy, and all the people who were so devoted to her for centuries. It all seemed so familiar that I burst into tears!

Yes Mary Magdalene had come calling. She had awakened the fire within me. And that fire would begin an unexpected and deeply passionate journey into a two-thousand-year-old story, one I could never ever have imagined would unfold before me!

But let me back up a moment because this is the part of the story that goes to timing of all kinds and destiny points in one's life.

I had seen all the Jesus movies growing up, including Martin Scorsese's 1988 film adaption of "*The Last Temptation of Christ*," based on the 1953 novel by Nikos Kazantzakis. This is the same writer who wrote "*Zorba the Greek*," which gained him international fame once the movie of the same name was released in 1964.

This movie was controversial when it was released in 1988; I remember going to see it. Mary Magdalene was played by Barbara Hershey. She won a Golden Globe for Best Supporting Actress for her performance. And Scorsese was nominated for an Academy Award for Best Director. But even with the story's possibilities and all the media attention it generated, it still hadn't stirred up the inspiration that was ignited in me in the year 2000.

Equally as strange was that I never heard about the book, first published in 1982, called "*The Holy Blood and the Holy Grail*," an international sensation that had caught the attention of the world! It put forth the idea that Jesus and Mary Magdalene were married and birthed a sacred bloodline. I don't know how that one didn't grab my attention. For whatever reason, it just wasn't in the cards at that time for me to take hold of this controversial information and run with it.

But in the year 2000, a year which bears the Roman numerals MM, my journey with this Mary would finally begin.

The more I researched, the more the uneasy feeling came over me that I had been lied to in my childhood, but not by my parents or even the local church we attended as a family. It was clear that the information which unfolded in my research was way beyond their scope of understanding.

And somewhere along the line, I began to read between the lines. The facts on Mary just didn't add up, especially her incredible legends in southern France. It seemed to me there was a vast cover-up of her true identity. And it had to come from the highest levels of power – a mighty and ancient power which could only come from the Vatican.

It was the same feeling I had when studying the assassination of President John F. Kennedy. The devil was in the details, and it made me sick to think another vast and complicated conspiracy was perpetrated on the world again. And yet, as complicated as that moment in American history was, it paled in comparison to the two thousand years of twisted history put forth by the Vatican.

The feeling of complete devotion that people have held for the Magdalene throughout time would become enshrined in my own devotion to her. I was deeply moved by her presence, but at the same time, emotionally conflicted by her story. And I mean deeply conflicted! The research threads were weaving together a fascinating tapestry, yet they were a far cry from accepted doctrine.

Through it all, I'm amazed that so many pieces came together. I was awash in details and memories that had a profound effect on me. My family was concerned with my obsession with Mary Magdalene, and the wild stories I shared with them. They were concerned about my changing beliefs, and by my undying passion for a saint of the first century. No one was excited about my revelations. In fact, their reaction was quite the contrary.

Before I knew it, a year had passed and my original play called "Magdalene's Mind" was completed. A theater friend of mine suggested I contact an old colleague of hers in New York City to see if he was interested in reading the play. Contact was made and we quickly decided a writing residency in the studio was a great place to start. Now this was in Manhattan, New York City, prior to 9/11. It was a less compassionate city back then, at least in my opinion.

The 9/11 event, with its terribly tragic underpinnings, seemed to open up the heart of New York City. Post 9/11, the world witnessed love and compassion between New Yorkers as they united and tried to make sense of what happened at the World Trade Center. But before this event, New York seemed very insensitive to me. And the theater studio highlighted that tough New York attitude. So, I piecemealed my script and worked with selected scenes, keeping its secret safe awhile longer.

The effect the dialogue was having on the actors was profound. Self-professed recovering Catholics were now telling me their stories during breaks. And others, not even knowing the outcome of the play, seemed to be getting personal messages as they recited their lines. It was crazy! They would end up either in shock or in tears by the mirror of the message to their own lives. Something was afoot in the studio but I wasn't sure what.

What I didn't realize back then, in early 2001, was that this phenomenon was the spirit of the Magdalene working her magic, way before the revelations in Dan Brown's *DaVinci Code* would take the world by storm!

⚜ ⚜ ⚜

While workshopping the play, I would take the train from Connecticut to Grand Central Station and make my way up to Columbus Circle, for my Saturday sessions with the other writers, directors and actors. It was an integrated group and we worked hard on improving our craft. After a full week's work, and then the studio work, needless to say, I was exhausted.

On the train ride back home, my emotions would overcome me. I shuddered to think what my mother would say of my play, were she alive. The guilt I felt by diligently following my truth and writing this full-length play was unbelievable.

In my play, "*Magdalene's Mind*," Mary appears in New York City, visiting unsuspecting native New Yorkers during the course of their day. These are imaginative encounters, and yet there is a palpable chemistry between Mary Magdalene and each character; her presence triggers them in unexpected ways. Each character – Sophia, Lydia and George – would never be the same after their encounter with Mary. And when her visits are done, Magdalene returns to Central Park. It's there that she hears her beloved in the park; he is looking for her. It is there, in that setting, that we see their relationship through modern eyes. It is there we feel the power of their presence together.

The play enjoyed success in the studio and was showcased with a handful of other new plays in a black box theater space in Times Square. It was also given a staged reading in Seattle in 2004, at a conference dedicated to Mary Magdalene. That is where I met Ani Williams and Margaret Starbird, some of my earliest sisters of the modern Magdalene Movement.

After that, my plan was to write another play on another woman in the bible. At least that's what I thought was the plan. Yet I couldn't seem to focus my efforts in that direction. I tried over and over again, to make that happen, but Magdalene and her Mysteries had completely captivated me.

Throughout these last thirteen years, I could not have imagined the journey before me, to learn of the Magdalene legends in faraway lands, including France, England, Scotland, Spain, and Egypt. I never thought that "holy grail" authors such as Dr. Tim Wallace-Murphy and Henry Lincoln would appear on my path and guide me with their astounding knowledge of esoteric history.

I remember hosting a conference in Connecticut in 2007 with Tom Kenyon, Judi Sion, William Henry and others. Tom was onstage and was sharing the story of how he came to be at this event, with the assistance of Ani Williams for the initial hook-up. With great emphasis, he declared that Magdalene's guidance was impeccable. I looked at Tom onstage and was humbled by his devotion to her. And when he told the audience that Magdalene informed him that I was truly "hearing" her voice, a radiant light washed over me. I had finally met someone who seemed to understand my experience because it was also his own.

Even with that incredible guidance, it has been a challenge all these years to try and explain this vast puzzle to people. Two thousand years of history is a lot to consider. There were times I just wanted to give up and go live my life in southwest France. Yet every time I asked for clarity, the answer would come that there was work to be done in the States. And apparently it was work that needed years of preparation, study, and contemplation, and some bigtime "crazy" along the way.

No matter how much I was stretched beyond my comfort zone, walking away was just not in the cards. It was imprinted on my soul in a way that defied time and place. No matter how bizarre people thought my life had become, I kept traveling. I kept researching, and I kept clearing personal beliefs that no longer served me. Sure, I've had my moments of self-doubt along the way but never any doubt in the immaculate tutelage of Mary Magdalene, and even Yeshua ben Yosef (Jesus). Their presence in my life was undeniable, even if their presence defied explanation.

I have come to learn that Mary Magdalene was a woman of extraordinary power and intelligence and that Yeshua considered her his equal. Unlike his contemporaries, Yeshua didn't seem to have a problem with women. Maybe it could be attributed to his exceptional relationship with his own mother. His embrace of the sacred feminine could also have evolved from his exposure to the cults of Isis which were prevalent in the Roman world during his time.

He also knew that the Holy Spirit was feminine in nature. It was Sophia, the goddess of wisdom. Jesus understood this essential wisdom; it would have been part of the teachings that guided him.

After all the years of walking with her, Mary Magdalene says she is ready to reveal certain details of her life with Yeshua. She has reminded me repeatedly that in order to "hear" her words, I would have to become a clear channel. And to that end, Mary would test me in ways I could never have imagined. Yet, despite the difficulties, I have tried my best to rise to that challenge.

Mary says that life is much more integrated today among people than it was in her time. In her revelations, there is much talk of initiation and she wants to be clear – that is how things were done in her day. Secrets had to be kept by those who respected their power.

This little book is a result of my conversations with Mary, of channeling her words as she has spoken them to me. Her presence is magical and moves me to a place of cosmic decree. Yet she is very earthy, and demands attention to detail. She says there are many revelations embedded in the smallest of details. As hard as it has sometimes been for me to understand those fine points, eventually they fall into place.

It has been an unexpected pilgrimage to walk with the Magdalene, but I am honored to stand beside her, year after year, and learn what I can from the light of her brilliance.

In my devotion to her, I have pledged perpetual pilgrimage – to travel the earth to herald her truth, over and over again, to eradicate the centuries of lies and distortions in her name.

Long live the Magdalene!

LIGHT FROM THE STARS

Chapter 2

LIGHT FROM THE STARS: AN EXPLANATION OF CHANNELING

O gather ye light from the stars, and place it in your heart…for the mind is full of starlight already…

Channeling is a process that has gained popularity in recent times. It requires your mind to be emptied of your thoughts and feelings as much as possible so you can align yourself with the vibration of someone or something else. That someone else usually resides in spirit form – whether it is a loved one who has crossed over, a spirit guide, or an ascended master. There are a variety of spirits you can connect with via channeling.

You can also connect with something called an oversoul consciousness. That's not the voice of an individual but rather a collective awareness. It's also possible to channel a different aspect of your being, something called the multidimensional aspect of the self.

Let's say I want to align to the voice of my guardian spirit. What I would do is clear my mind of all thoughts best I could and breathe deeply for a few minutes, forgetting my concerns and becoming very present with my awareness. I want to establish a dialogue with a consciousness and can usually do this without speaking aloud – just relaxing and connecting with that wavelength. It's like turning the dial on the radio until you stop at a station and listen for awhile.

It's a good practice to identify who or what energy you're linking to during this process. I simply ask who it is that wishes to speak through me. They must be clear. And if I choose to bring that energy through me, then the channeling begins. However, just like humans, entities or spirits can be tricky at times. It's best to start slowly and be mindful of what consciousness you're merging with when you channel because energies that flow through your body will affect you.

Once I'm confident the proper connection has been made with my guardian spirit, in this case Mary Magdalene, I again breathe slowly and deliberately, clearing my mind even more. I must become an empty vessel waiting to be filled with her spirit.

Trust is the key and that takes time. Be patient and know, like anything else, the more you practice this technique, the more you channel, the better it gets.

Channeling was well-established in the ancient world and even into modern day. As the western mind shifted into exclusive left-brain functioning, outward society decided it was lunacy or delusion that propelled someone into this right-brained state of consciousness. Yet, in secret, this practice has been prevalent among those who wish to experience the Mysteries more fully.

At least now, with more awakened minds on the planet, and with scientific research merging with spiritually, we're rediscovering the extraordinary power of the right brain. This part of our brain is intuitive and creative and when used properly, exudes an amazing intelligence that I have found to far supersede the limitations of left-brained critical and analytical thinking.

Don't get me wrong. Left-brained thinking has its place. But its total domination over our entire being is coming to an end. Even technology is becoming more intuitive.

The American government is fascinated with the mysteries of right-brained faculties, although they continually try to weaponize it. They understand the innate power of the human pineal gland. They've even used the right-brained activity known as remote viewing. Google it. You'll find stories of psychic phenomena being used for espionage purposes.

Quite honestly, do you think our Creator, with all the divine proportions designed within us, would have given us a third eye, or pineal gland, in our body for no reason? The simple answer is no. It is there for a purpose. When it's activated and nurtured, it can facilitate our psychic abilities in ways we are beginning to master once again.

When I first aligned with the spirit of Mary Magdalene, it was an overpowering frequency that rocked my world. But through clearing unprocessed emotion and thus liberating my vibration, I experienced an expanded bandwidth, and have become a much clearer channel. I began hearing her voice much more easily, with much less shock to my nervous system.

In March 2013 the presence known as Mary Magdalene came to me and said I would need to undergo another shift in consciousness in order to receive some new information from her. I agreed, not really knowing how that would play out or what she was up to, but trusting that things would unfold exactly as they should. And over the course of a few weeks, her words came true. I dug even deeper, and in that process, cultivated more "open space" and clarity within me.

The channeling in this book is a reflection of receiving her inspired teachings, which sometimes has included shocking revelations of her time here on earth.

Mary says it is time to lift the veil to the Mysteries. In that spirit, she offers her words of wisdom for your consideration. In these next two chapters are contained tenets of alchemy, metaphysics and universal laws. Also included are some Teachings of the Way.

Her words are short in pages and long in energies that can vibrate to the core of your being. Allow these words to work their magic on you and see what happens. Feel the depth of her soul.

If you read this book with an open mind, her words *will* find their place in your heart...

THE VESSEL

Chapter 3

THE VESSEL: MAGDALENE'S MEMOIR

Below is an account of Magdalene's memoir, as told to me by her.

"My early training is not known in your world because it would not have been understood in your world, at least until now. The Mysteries were secretive even when I was born, although the desire to understand such things stirred in my soul since I took my first breath.

When I was a child I was in unison with the natural world. My mother taught me about the cycles of the earth and my father taught me about the cycles of the stars in the heavens. They instilled in me a deep and abiding sense of the sacred in our world – from the olive trees to the salted waters to the potency of the prophecies of the Ancient Ones.

My father always said to look to the heavens, for there God's plan would unfold.

My mother always said to look to the earth – for there our fruit would manifest accordingly.

❦ ❦ ❦

For me there was always a sense of wonder for the plants and the birds and the whispers on the wind. I could read the elements of the natural world very clearly. I knew when it would rain and when the sun would come out again. I knew when the serpent of the earth would snake across the land, and when it was time for the land to lay fallow.

There was great power that moved within all that sprung from the natural world. My mother taught me to embrace this power. She taught me how to harness this power for the benefit of our people. But she was clear with me that in order for it to be considered beneficial to us, it had to serve the land as well. It had to serve the plants and animals, and all the beneficent beings.

Even at a very young age, my mother said my clarity of mind was exceptional. She was resolute with father that I needed to be educated in the temple. I listened carefully to her and obeyed her every word; she was everything to me. I loved my father and my siblings dearly, truly I did, but my mother was the sun and the moon and the stars; she was my All.

My initiations began as I played in the intense heat and sought shelter in the caves in our native landscape. It was there in those caves I began to understand the depth of our world. It was in the caves that the Ancient Ones came to me and told me the creational stories of our planet. They were wondrous stories that made me laugh and dance with delight.

Sometimes my brother would come with me, but when he did, the Ancient Ones would hide from him. When I would go alone, they would appear. I would bring gifts for them, like rocks and figures made of sticks. I laid a fine cloth on the ground, one from mother's basket of colorful linens. I would arrange a small altar in honor of their coming and sing the songs they taught me. They were simple songs but their melodies were from the heavens. The notes were inspired by the breath of the angels. The singing would always make them appear, right on time.

Sometimes I would fall asleep in the caves, away from the blazing sun of the desert. My mother would worry when I was gone for too long and send my brother and his friends to find me. But the Ancient Ones cradled me with fierce protection. They always said no harm would come to me ever, for my destiny required that to be so.

Later I will reveal what the Ancient Ones showed me in the caves. It is truly magical. For now, I will tell you this. When the time came for me to learn more, they gave me very specific instructions, ones I was to pass on to mother. They said if she did not believe me, they would appear to her and make things clear. But my mother, being the wise-woman she was, did not doubt me. To this day, I am grateful for her steadfast devotion to my soul's purpose.

✣ ✣ ✣

FORMAL TRAINING

The day I said goodbye to my family was one of the hardest in my life. My mother had a deep understanding of what I was to learn and study. It required rigorous devotion and we agreed the temple was the place for me to receive that most stringent instruction.

The Ancient Ones had instructed me to go to the land of Egypt. They insisted that to work with the Mysteries there would give me the comprehensive understanding I needed for what was to come. It was their emphasis of the nine bodies of light that was to be the focus of my attention. It was told to me that I was to master this understanding so that when the time came, I could teach the One. And so I set off for the place of High Magic. It was there I would learn of immortality, and of the communication between not only the living and the dead, but between starlight and soil.

When I arrived in the golden land of Khem, I was met by someone whom my mother had met long before my arrival there. She knew him well and had arranged for him to be my guide and guardian. My mother wanted to be certain that while my training was ongoing, there was someone there who could watch over me, and make sure that I was receiving proper instruction.

So there I was, so in love with the natural world and so ready for the secrets of the Mysteries to be revealed to me. As my guardian and I walked the streets together, he pointed out many things, from practical matters of the market and safety, to the spectacular gold and jeweled objects that were a young girl's dream. I was mesmerized by the riches that could be found everywhere in the markets. It was dazzling and exotic and I loved every minute of it!

There is much to speak of about my temple training. To say it was an education is an understatement. It was everything I had dreamed it could be, but it was so much more than I could ever have imagined. It encompassed the light from the stars. But it also held much darkness – and from where it came, I did not know. Even to this day, you do battle with this evil on your beautiful earth. More will be revealed about this darkness, as will my preparation for what was to come. But I will share the following experience. All I can say is – draw from it what you will.

It was a particularly hot day, even for Egypt, so the idea of going deep into the underground where it was cool and quiet, seemed a very good one. I had passed many of my initiations and was feeling quite confident that mother would be well pleased with my progress. After my morning duties, I decided to descend deep into my temple, and find a cool, peaceful spot to take a much-needed nap. I passed by those who were familiar to me, exchanging the customary temple greeting to one another. Then I stopped by the underground pool, and sat for awhile, cupping and streaming my hands through the water. It seemed such a luxury and I admit my delight on feeling so good, so young and so accomplished. I missed my family, and mother most of all, but I was eager to learn all that I could during my training.

I decided to descend deeper still into the temple. There were less people moving about as I walked down the stairs and made my way to the final layer of sand and earth in the temple complex. If there were more levels, they were hidden to me.

At some point, I realized there was no one down there. I was alone. And I began to wonder what went on in the depths of this space. In the distance I could hear voices. They were unfamiliar and sounded abrasive, so I decided it best to hide from them.

As they approached, my heart beat faster. When they passed by me, they stopped and looked around, as if they sensed my presence. But seeing no one, and perhaps used to seeing no one this far down, they resumed their pace and their conversation.

Once I felt sure they had gone to another chamber, I stepped out from the shadows and could see something shining in the distance. Could it be the Ancient Ones?

I was not prepared for what would come next.

I watched as a beautiful young woman was escorted against her will by two guards. She was protesting their hold on her and crying at the same time.

I looked over to the shining light in the distance, hoping it was one of my spirit guardians. The light was faint but steady and it seemed to be hovering. I slowly and quietly walked closer to the chamber where the guards had taken the young woman. It was a large and imposing hall, and the ceremonial fires were lit. It was clear some sort of ritual was taking place but what? And what were their intentions with this temple maiden?

Then the customary temple chanting began, and the vibrations from their voices were bringing the stones alive. There was movement and shaking and ritual incantation. I could smell the frankincense and the burning of human hair. And then the young woman started to scream.

When I looked down into the great chamber, I could see a being. He was large and lizard like, and not of this world! The young woman was continuing to fight and resist their advances. I stepped back and tried to think of what to do. It seemed almost foolish to barge into the room and plead for her release but it's what I wanted to do. Just as I was about to step inside, the light that appeared to me deep inside the temple hovered in front of me and rendered me motionless.

All I can remember after that was being awakened from my slumber by the pool of water I had earlier run through my fingers. A gentleman of the temple, one who I recognized from my daily tasks, was calling to me to wake up and return to my station, that it soon would be time to start preparing for the evening meal. I was in shock at what I had seen, but could not figure out if it was a dream or if it was real. It certainly felt real. I remembered seeing the light that hovered around me in the dream while I was in the bowels of the temple. That felt real too.

I dusted myself off and made my way back up to the main temple. Everyone seemed to be moving slowly, the alarming heat of the day still greatly oppressive.

I spoke of my afternoon experience with no one. I had always heard the whispers in the halls about young girls disappearing in broad daylight from the temple and the insatiable sexual desires of some of the elders of the priesthood, but I dismissed it as gossip. Now I wondered if there really could be some truth to these rumors. And what of the lizard like man in the bowels of the temple? Was that my imagination or did these creatures linger there, deep underground? And what were they doing with the young maidens from the temple?

After that event, I made myself blend into my surroundings rather than stand out. I studied hard and finished all my initiations, and there were many. I prepared myself to leave the day my training had come to an end. I requested my guardian get a message to my family to meet me on my last day in temple and then leave immediately thereafter.

Whatever I witnessed on that hot summer's day changed me. I did notice certain young women went missing after that day, but I did not speak of it. Who would I tell and who would believe what I saw when I wasn't even sure if it was a dream or a real experience?

The Ancient Ones had come to me after that day and explained to me that I was shown the dark side of my experience so that I could begin to understand the powers of creation – both light and dark, especially ones who were under the spell of Enki. But their clarification left me even more confused than before, so I blocked the whole affair from my mind the best I could.

In keeping with the promise the Ancient Ones made to me, no harm came my way while in the temple. But knowing such evil walked so closely by me every day, made me cringe. I knew that my light was strong and growing steadily, but their darkness disturbed me nonetheless. And for all the innocent victims who were brought to the bowels of the temple, seemingly never to return to us, I was more determined than ever to rise to the highest level of spiritual mastery and ascend into the light. At least by doing so, I could one day reclaim their souls.

LEAVING THE TEMPLE

It was my last day in the temple. I was eager to be reunited with my family. Yet I had a tremendous sense of foreboding on this day. When my guardian came to get me, he had a frightened look on his face. He was very pale and uneasy. I asked him if he was feeling alright, and he nodded. But he was unconvincing. We gathered my things. Then he took me to his family's quarters, where my brother and one of our servants were waiting for me. This was not the welcome I expected.

"Where is mother?" I immediately asked Lazarus.

"Miriam," he began. "There-"

"Where is she? Where is father?"

"There has been a terrible accident." What was Lazarus saying to me? "Miriam…sit down."

I started to tremble. "Where is mother? Are they not with you?"

"No Miriam, they are not."

"Why?"

"They are gone."

"Gone"

"Yes."

"Gone where?"

"To their Maker, Miriam. They are no longer with us."

"No! That cannot be!" I screamed out.

"It is true. They are gone."

I was inconsolable. Lazarus tried his best but it was no use. I just could not imagine my life without my parents. I am told my crying went on for days. Finally Lazarus decided it was time to make the journey back to our family home.

I didn't want to go, but I didn't want to stay where I was. I cared not to go on any longer, and told my brother of my feelings. He sternly reminded me that mother did not send me to Egypt to have such a careless attitude about my calling. But my heart was shattered into so many pieces. How could I go back now and live in our family home without mother and father? The thought of it was unbearable. Why had this happened to them? And what would become of us?

ON THE WAY HOME

It was an exhausting trip back home. My training at temple had come to its finish, and it was time to begin a new chapter of my life. I had memorized all the incidents I wished to discuss with mother and all the questions I intended to ask her. There were so many things I experienced that needed her wise counsel. There was so much yet for me to learn from her. But that was not to be.

On the way up the road to our estate in Bethany, people were gathered, offering their support in our family's time of grief. My eyes were so swollen from crying and all the dust on the journey home. They were so red and sore. And I hadn't washed my face in days. It was filthy. I must have looked like a terrible sight to all these kind people.

I wanted to run away, or at least hide my face from them. I wanted my privacy. I wanted to be left alone! Lazarus reached out and put his arm on my shoulder and pointed with the other one. I could see a small group of people huddled off to the side of the road, up ahead. There was a radiance surrounding them. They looked vaguely familiar.

As we drew closer to where they stood, I saw Miriam, Yeshua's mother. Her eyes were filled with such sadness. And then I turned and saw Yeshua himself. I hadn't seen him in years. Our studies had taken us both in separate directions, to faraway places – Yeshua to southern France and Britain and even India. And me – to the golden lands of Egypt!

I turned away, embarrassed by my physical condition. As much as I was grieving, I still felt that sensation in my body – the feeling you get when you are deeply attracted to someone.

Yeshua looked at me with his piercing eyes. It was like laser light penetrating my soul. He was even more handsome since the last time I saw him. My mind was racing with so many thoughts and feelings all at once that I collapsed into my brother's arms, only to be later awakened in my bed by Yeshua himself!

"Miriam, wake up," he called out to me. "Your time has not come to leave this world. There is much for you to do on earth, and much we are to do together," he said as he smiled at me.

I couldn't believe I was hearing these words. It was all too much. To lose my parents and be without my mother was heart-wrenching, then to have Yeshua sitting at the foot of my bed, talking softly to me while the others looked on from a distance. It was like a dream-come-true emerging from my nightmare! I looked into his beautiful eyes, eyes so full of light, and could sense spiritual maturity had come over him. He reached for my hand with his, and held it for the longest time.

I cannot tell you what happened next, not at this time, because it is so deeply personal and so hard to believe. And yet, there were a handful of us who witnessed it. In time I will reveal the details.

But I will say it had to do with what you call the sacred heart and the energies that can radiate from an illumined heart center. This teaching, he would later tell me, came from the East.

On that day Yeshua touched my heart in a way that no man had ever done before. And in my fragile state, the fear arose in me that I would cling to him too much. My fierce independence had gone missing during my time of grief. I was vulnerable to everything that came my way.

Yeshua did not care what anyone else thought of his intimate gestures. He held me tight and told me in time I would come to understand the timing of my parents' tragedy. He said they had gone on to the Creator, for their work here on earth, especially with their children, was finished. That's why they died together, he said. They had incarnated with the calling to be our parents and to teach us from their combined wisdom. And they had fulfilled their destinies.

Yeshua said I had to be brave because there were many trials and tribulations ahead of us. "This is the way of mastery, Miriam. This is the course of events for us now. We must find a way to allow the tenderness of our touch to lead us to our true path together. We are no longer children Miriam. We will need each other now more than ever. You will see."

And with that, he got up and left my side. I didn't know where he was going but I could hear him leaving the house. Martha came with Mary, and they sat by my side, feeding me bits and pieces of food, and washing the dirt from my face. They tended to my eyes with healing plants, and soon I felt soothed and comforted by their care.

"Dear child, you must get some rest. My son has gone to recharge himself so that when he returns, he can administer the light transmission to you. He will lay his hands upon you and heal your wounds. There is much you need to know."

And with those words, these two gifted, strong women delicately washed and caressed me, and consoled me with their sweet songs. Martha sometimes could not feel so easily, so I was her mirror for the emotions she held deep within her. But Mary – she was a compassionate soul who could heal everyone around her with her radiant smile. She looked at me for hours on end, a look that said I was safe and loved, and despite everything that happened, life would continue.

YESHUA'S NIGHT WITH THE STARS

My focus was starting to return, if even a little. Martha and Mary continued to watch over me, although I could see Martha growing impatient with my sadness. She refrained from speaking plainly to me about it since Mary was there and we had other house guests. But soon, my sister Martha would return to her stern ways with me. She loved me dearly. I knew that. But she was always the more responsible one, and sometimes she got angry with me for not being like her. She worked from dawn to dusk. Mother saw something different in me from a very young age and I think sometimes Martha resented that. But I loved my sister and would always comb her hair every night before bed and tell her how much I loved her. I asked her forgiveness for my ways but told her it was my destiny to study and learn so that one day I could be a great teacher to my people.

Many days passed before Yeshua would return to me. I longed to see him, but sensed we were both being prepared for something, although what that was, I did not know. After the second day, I got up from the bed and began to walk about my bedroom. I even sat by the window and felt the warm rays of the sun. I could hear the birds chirping outside.

And I could hear this man's soul calling out to me in the night. It was an eerie sound, as if he was being tempted by demon spirits. At times he seemed to be in agony, and other times in ecstasy. It was hard to explain how I could not see him for so long, but upon my return from Egypt, it was as if an instantaneous thread was woven between us.

I learned how to travel the inner worlds while at temple, but this time was different. I could only go so far and get just so close to Yeshua's circle in the sand. This was his spiritual initiation and I was to be a bystander in this process. And what I witnessed was just earth-shaking. With all I had seen in the temples of Egypt, this was by far, a most incredible revelation.

Yeshua was in the process of receiving a light transmission from the star Sirius. I kid you not! He knew how to connect to the stars directly and receive the codes of creation that each star carries for our spiritual evolution here on earth.

As I have said before, our world is created by the resonance of numbers and the harmonies they generate. And the concert of such harmony in numbers comes from the light codes that shine from the stars. These harmonies undulate like the serpentine waves that have been with us since the beginning. The waves pulse their wisdom through the heavens, onto the land, and into the earth, awakening the layers of our memory according to our understanding.

I had witnessed this process in the King's Chamber of the Great Pyramid. It was a powerful sequence of events the initiate had to pass through in order to connect with that star-gate. But that Yeshua could do it in the wide open all by himself was a testament to his strength, both physical and spiritual. He commanded the stars to unfurl their magic and reach down to him, swirl inside of him, and exit with an array of colors not of this world!

When one opens these gates, one must fend off the darker spirits that reside around the rim of the circular opening. One must be an accomplished soul to be able to do this and not allow the dark forces to enter into your field of light.

So on that night, I sat by the window and stared at the starry skies, sending my love to Yeshua, opening my heart to this most accomplished man. I cried as he released energies that had come to their natural end within him, and watched in amazement when his genetic material activated within his body. It was as if there was a lightning storm inside of him, and my tears were part of the rain that would wash away the dark charges of any destructive forces that tried to infiltrate his circle.

From my bedroom window, I traveled through time and stayed with him all night in the desert. I had learned these techniques during my training and could assist him in this way. My body was sitting on the edge of my bedroom window, but my spirit soared with him on this night.

It would be up to him to survive his ordeal and make his way back to my family's home – a place he had known so well as a boy. Exhausted and weary, I felt my anima had served him well. So I crawled back to my bed and fell asleep just as the sun was rising.

It would be three days before I would recover from this experience.

YESHUA'S RETURN

I woke up to the sounds of clucking chickens and excited voices. Before I could fully open my eyes, Martha entered my bedroom to tell me Yeshua had returned from the desert. She said I best be getting up and making myself presentable to him.

He said when he returned, our private talks would begin. So the time had come for me to put aside my grief, at least long enough to hear what he had to say to me. I was still devastated by the loss of my parents and missed mother terribly.

It had been so many years since we sat under the stars as children and envisioned the heavens with such wonder. It had been an eternity that we ran through the wheat fields and laughed with wild abandon. It seemed like lifetimes ago that my childhood dreams of spending my life with Yeshua and our families kept me awake at night imagining the details.

Everything changed when I went to Egypt. The formal training was so demanding at times, but then other times I would have days on end to reflect on the outcome of initiations and what they meant to me. My worldview had changed. My innocence was taken from me in a way that I had not expected. I was required to do things I did not understand and witness things I did not like. And I was not allowed to question authority, but simply to obey, whether I thought something was right or wrong. My elders said there was a chain of command and I was to follow it. At first I resisted and was punished severely for it, so I succumbed to the temple rules. But I swore when my studies were completed, I would develop my own teachings. I respected temple wisdom but knew there were cosmic forces that could teach me even more. I trusted the vibration of the land and all the elements that the Creator had given us. These were aspects of the light and they held a cosmic harmony that even the temple, in all its glory, could not reproduce on earth.

I took Martha's advice and cleaned myself in preparation for my time with Yeshua. Martha laid out some of my finer clothing for me. Mother would always do that on special occasions. She always laughed with delight when I paraded through the house with the special outfits she had chosen for me. I think Martha was sometimes put off by our behavior, but she was close to father, and I accepted that bond between them. Still, there was always tension with Martha. And yet, here she was, putting out my clothes for me. I didn't know whether to laugh or cry.

I could hear Yeshua laughing that belly laugh of his – hearty and loud and absolutely contagious. He laughed like that even when he was a little boy. When you would hear it, even if you couldn't see him, there was no mistaking who it was!

I combed my hair and draped it to one side. Then I finished dressing. I recognized some of mother's exquisite linen scarves that Martha had laid on the bed for me. They were made with the finest threads money could buy. Covering myself in all of them, I emerged from my quarters and made my way into the kitchen, where Martha was preparing a celebration feast now that Yeshua had returned.

He turned and smiled at me. It was a smile that told me he was very happy to see me, and that he noticed me as a woman. It made me blush. He was such a sensual man. It was embedded in the way he moved, the way he spoke, the way he thought. He was such a mixture of opposites. One moment he was so playful and kind, then the next he would look at me with his commanding way and my heart would skip a beat!

Martha would not let me help her in the kitchen. I don't really blame her. She was a wonderful cook, and I, well, not so much. So I stood back and listened to Yeshua tell Lazarus and his mother the story of where he had gone and what had been revealed to him. Much to my amazement, he included me in the story. He clearly knew I traveled in my spirit body to be with him on that night. Lazarus seemed a little confused, but Mary understood him completely. She turned to me and smiled a somewhat hesitant smile, as if she knew what lay before us in the world. I'm not sure how she could have known these things, but Mary the Mother was someone who was always ten steps ahead of everyone, as if she could see the future as easily as she saw the present moment.

❧ ❧ ❧

That afternoon, after resting from the magnificent feast Martha had prepared, Yeshua asked me to walk outside with him. He said this in front of everyone so they would know where we were going. When Lazarus got up to join us, Yeshua said in an authoritative voice – "Miriam and I must speak alone, dear brother. But before we do, I wish you to witness my mother and I clearing Miriam of the dark spirits that came to her during my night with the stars."

Yeshua explained once again how I had been with him in spirit, and how I took on some of the dark forces that tried to penetrate his circle of light on that night. He told them that he could see some of those spirits had attached to me, given my weakened state. In my vulnerability, he said, these demon spirits attached to me, in the seven primary energy centers in my spirit body.

And so, with Yeshua in front of me and Mother Mary behind me, Martha and Lazarus and a few others watched on as Yeshua directed them to leave my body. There were strange noises and apparently I was writhing in pain as the spirits flew from me and towards the light.

I was awestruck at his imposing voice! And I encountered some powerful magicians during my time in Egypt. But Yeshua's command was different. There was clarity and fierceness to the cadence of his voice. When he spoke our native tongue, he had the ability to instruct the life-force. It sent chills up and down my spine. My light body was cleansed of the dark spirits that overcame me on his night with the stars. It was a relief to have my energy field aligned once again. At a different time, I would have recognized this immediately. But given the state of shock I was in, it didn't surprise me that this had happened. What did surprise me was how powerful Yeshua had grown from his training.

Now I understood why we needed to talk privately. I knew he sensed in me an equally powerful spiritual adept, even in my compromised state. And his mother knew our time together was drawing near. So she assured everyone that what they witnessed was real and was a testament to our mission together on earth.

Yeshua and I walked for awhile without saying a word. It's as if we were communicating in a different way with each other, through our minds. And the sparks of the sacred heart between us were so overwhelming that we both needed to stop and breathe along the way. We managed to laugh about it. But we did not take it lightly. We knew something special had ignited between us!

After a few hours, we settled down enough to find a comfortable spot and sit down. We remained in view of the others, so that they could see us at all times. Yeshua had great respect and love for my family, and as much as he was rebellious, he would never disrespect my family or his dear mother. He loved to play practical jokes on her but he loved her from a place in his heart that is rarely seen between a mother and her grown son. It would take your breath away to see him with her, and see how they talked with each other.

When we sat down, we faced each other. Yeshua said he wanted to see the light in my eyes and feel my heart beating in unison with his. I was falling in love with him all over again. It brought back memories of when we were little, when the idea of loving him was a girlish thought in my childhood mind. But here I was, an accomplished woman of the temple with a vast knowledge of the Mysteries. If there were any doubts I may have had of my time in Egypt, they were all washed away in this moment, when we looked into each other's eyes. We knew we had come together to leave our mark on the world for many generations to come.

We knew that beyond the suffering that lay ahead for us, and for so many to come, that when the great cycle of time had ended, the world would look back on our story and begin to understand the revelation of our achievement together, which was spiritual freedom from the bondage of the ego. I cannot stress this enough to you!

Time and again it would be my training that would bring order and ability to my fluttering romantic heart, and discipline to the chaos that was to come. And for his part, Yeshua knew that I was the one person in this world, along with his mother, who completely understood his mission and our parts in it. We were a holy trinity, the three of us.

The starlight that had come to Yeshua on that night was the light of Sophia, as she comes by the moon, especially the full moon. That transmission of light is something we train our bodies to withstand, after proper preparation of fasting and purification, and singing the sacred songs.

The great and mysterious dove of the waters is the union of that starlight with the pineal gland in the human brain. It is designed to comprehend those light waves in a way that you still do not remember, but you will come to understand more fully in the very near future.

That Mother Mary was a prodigy of the temple in her day was an understatement. That Yeshua would be born from her ancestral memories is a most beautiful rendering of this bond between a mother and child. But it was not emphasized in that way. Rather it was twisted to fabricate a divine birth, just like those of ancient Egypt.

The truth of his birth is that it was a human birth. There were so many in the community that helped prepare Mary for this child's birth. It was amazing. When he was in Mary's belly, she was already telling him the ancient stories of creation here on earth. And she was already opening the sacred heart energy within him.

Mary told a funny story of how she would tell the stories of our spiritual lineage and ask if he could hear her. She would say "move your legs and kick your feet if you hear me little one." And sure enough he would. Mary also said when she would animate the stories to Yeshua, her belly would shake all over. That was how close they were from the very beginning.

And I, the woman he called his equal, his reflection in this world, would eventually come to understand all those strange and difficult things I experienced in Egypt. My mother had chosen well for me, with the help of the Ancient Ones. For it led me to a broadened worldview. I'm not saying I liked it, but it helped me understand the choices we had to make along the way, choices that would seem strange to so many. But Yeshua knew I understood those choices. He knew I saw far beyond the village and the tribe, and far into the future, just like he did. That we consulted with great wise ones who understood the movement of the stars and the completion of the cycles, was a given.

As I have said before, the real magic was in our light-bodies and how they ignited each other. The flame of the twins burned brightly before us. And in the fires of our own conjunction, we knew our destinies were inseparable.

We practiced the rituals and recited the incantations to grow our light. We sat with the rays of the sun in the morning and at midday. Then we danced on hallowed ground by the sacred fires and sang to the stars at night. We breathed in particles of light as if we were ingesting the nectar of the gods. We observed the honeybees and watched the precision of pollination. How they gathered what they needed from the flowers, was an understanding we used in our practice. This knowledge would help us spread the words of truth that we had cultivated from deep within us.

The time had come to break the temple code and silence, and teach him of my knowledge. He had traveled far and wide and had learned much through his uncle Joseph. His travels in Britain connected him to the Druids and their incredible body of knowledge. That is a story in itself, and one I will address later on. It was there he learned many of the secrets of the Mysteries.

Yeshua also knew that he must reveal the fullness of the Mysteries, as only he knew them. He went through these teachings step by step with me. He was overjoyed that I was a quick learner. And he loved learning the details of the cosmic teachings from Khem.

Once we accomplished this, it was our task to walk among the people and cultivate an inner circle of disciples, to share the secret teachings so they could be learned and wisely passed on. We had to be careful for what we were teaching was a threat to the powers that be. We emphasized direct experience and that threatened all authorities at that time, not just the priesthood. That it was easier for Yeshua to travel and teach was a given. But my own discomfort did not stop me from my mission. There were times of great threat to me but the Ancient Ones were always there. They protected me all the days of my earthly life, just like they said they would.

That it has taken so long for the world to see a glimpse of our light together is but a moment in time from where we now stand. We are glad recognition is coming, not because we want it, but because it is a signal to us that you are finally ready to embrace the creational light within yourselves.

And that brings me to another subject altogether.

In this time, it is up to you to make a choice, to embrace the starlight within you. I have talked about it before and must stress that it is this light within you that Yeshua perfected. He came to a place within where all the Mysteries take hold and propel you forward to your counterparts from the stars. It is a transfiguration of the light, and a merging with the beings of light that seeded this world from the very beginning. It is as if they sent a light ray from their essence to earth and have waited all this time – until the cycles of time supported the great awakening – so they could step into their prepared earth body. In other words, they prepared us to become them, so that they could walk the earth once again in physical form.

During our time on earth, we knew what we were seeding, and we knew the darkness we were up against. But we also held a deep understanding of our mission and that it would eventually come to fruition, as the evolution of all living things accelerated in time.

One of the reasons our time on earth was so mysteriously and erroneously recorded was that there were certain details that could not be revealed. There were secret traditions that we cultivated with our trusted inner circles in many places throughout far and distant lands.

Just as many of you are realizing, we knew the overlay of potent lines of energy in the earth could be infused with thought-forms. We understood how the land and the waters carried the sounds of creation, and how these same sounds were encoded in our prayers and incantations.

We understood so much more than history has taught you. And we know many of you are angry because of the deception and the lies. But we ask you to consider that if it were told to your ancestors in the past, unless it was in secret, the knowledge would have been used by those who were living as Dark Ones. They ruled upon the earth in so many heinous ways and their actions had to take their course. But now, with your turning towards the light, all they have done, and are still doing to this day, will soon be exposed for the evil that it is.

The Dark Ones understand the cycles of time have shifted. So in their remaining days on earth, they will try anything and everything to deceive you and even torment you. You must not turn away from this ugliness but rather acknowledge this force is active in your world.

Shine your inner light directly into their eyes and make them see and feel the light of truth for they cannot withstand it! This is why you are here in such great numbers right now. This was deliberate planning by the creational forces and is why the children are being born with their cellular matrix already prepared to hold more light than ever before. Yes, there is strength in numbers.

This is not the time for inaction. Yes, your world has turned the corner and is making its way to the celestial light. But how you get there – by grace or by violent upheaval – is your destiny. The steps so many of you have already taken, especially in these last twenty-five years, was to purify yourselves of the dogma and conditioning that the Dark Ones had used on you with great success.

You must understand that they will reap what they have sown. They will be given a chance to leave this planet through the periphery of the gate of stars that is opening soon for them to pass through. It will be a mass exodus and souls will go with them.

Do not be fooled by their false proclamations.

Know it will be what is required to shift the planet to the light reception in a fuller capacity.

The light has always been within us. Yeshua repeated that over and over again. But no one ever told you how to turn that light on and keep it on. No one ever told you, until now.

(But why now, you ask? There is cosmic protection available for you now. Your alignment with the center of the Milky Way galaxy commands authority at this time. It is part of the changing of cycles. That is how the power is shifting. And it is a most glorious thing!)

When Yeshua and I came together in Bethany we discussed many things. We knew that there were channels of energy running throughout our bodies and to activate these channels, was to activate the Creator God within us.

That's why, when I took on the demon spirits during Yeshua's night with the starlight, he had to clear me of those entities. They were blocking the way of the light, some by design and some by sheer desperation to find their way back to Creation. Often they are terrified due to their heinous deeds while on earth. And there were many heinous crimes perpetuated against us and others who were connected to us, whether by blood or by the activation of our ancestral memories.

The ancestral memories are like turning on a supercomputer inside of us and letting it run unimpeded. Could you imagine what it would be like if we could run at a full capacity – both with our brains and our hearts? There is vast intelligence waiting to be released within our bloodstream, carrying super oxygen, or memory, to the very cells of our being.

It is this memory that gives us access to the entire records of our time here on earth. It is an incredible story that was not to be known in the precarious times of the past. Look at how you have harnessed that energy into destructive weapons that could annihilate the earth!

But as you transition between the worlds of darkness and confusion and into the blinding light of the age to come, you are making internal transitions so you can withstand the photons that are bombarding your world at this time.

In my inner circles, I would clear the emotional patterning that held back initiates. Then a sacred dance would be performed around them, utilizing vast earth forces. This allowed for the energy centers of the body to swirl and move the wheels of light into alignment with Creation.

After the initiate integrated that experience, Yeshua would stand before them and breathe into them the geometries of light that came from the stars. Some might call this the Book of Love in its organic form. If the initiate could integrate this transmission, then we would have merged their polarized energies into a unified field. It wasn't easy but we did accomplish it!

We performed these activations in secret so the prevailing authorities did not know what we were up to. We kept it quiet for some time and were able to bring many people to this state of conscious awareness. As a result, they all were responsible for harmonizing the songlines of the earth – of sending forth the sacred incantations and maintaining the integrity of these lines of force.

Many of these devoted disciples understood the mission and endured tremendous hardship to complete their work. They also had a duty to pass on these teachings and perform the Great Work within the human body, and within the earth. This was a great communion of energy and it was practiced on every continent.

After this work was completed, Yeshua and I began to realize, that in the very dark times to come, we would be much more powerful and reach many more by ascending into a collective awareness on earth so we could assist many more in their transition.

It would be a way to keep the light alive, and then assist in the great awakening of this time.

And so we chose, through different methods, and at different times, to make our ascension into a permanent state of being, one the alchemists throughout time have strived to embody.

It all goes full circle to ancient Egypt. Their fascination with the stars was well recorded. The secret teachings taught us, if we were diligent in our training, that it was possible we could become an emissary of the stars in the fullness of time.

Our molecular structure is set up for this transition but it takes a pure and devout heart to reach this state of gnosis. Mother Mary understood this process well. She was a star being come alive in a most extraordinary way!

So, this is some of what we did to prepare you for the light transition.

❖ ❖ ❖

You may ask yourselves why we came so early on in the process, nearly 2000 years before the migration of souls could be enacted. Yet I can assure that we came to be born right on time!

Changing the matrix of consciousness upon this dense planet is a massive undertaking. That it took this long for humanity to evolve to where it is today, is no surprise. And it is obvious that we have a ways to go before enough of you truly claim your spiritual lineage. That lineage is the power bestowed upon all of us in human form.

This was part of our calling – to remind you of your legacy.

Your legacy is to renew your spiritual power and teach your brothers and sisters how to do this, too, for there is strength in numbers. And there are many at this time willing to participate in the Dance of Light, to become galvanized peacemakers in your world."

THE SEALS HAVE
OPENED

Chapter 4

THE SEALS HAVE OPENED: MARY'S ANSWERS

In this chapter, these questions were posed to Mary Magdalene in channeled sessions. The questions are in bold; what follows are her answers.

What was the connection between Egypt and Atlantis?

The connection between Egypt and Atlantis was odd. Egypt was a land steeped in visceral power and a worshipping of the elements through deity. Their preoccupation with celestial gold was unparalleled. Why they focused so much on that had much to do with the location of Giza Plateau and the incredible power it radiated throughout the land, and even the entire planet.

Atlantis was a different culture with different goals. Atlantis was about magnifying energy and thought through the use of master crystals, harvested from deep within the earth. It was about using the memory from these crystals and creating an advanced society for its people. It was very much a cerebral place, and certainly an outstanding one.

Egypt was a raw power generator and more crass than Atlantis. Atlantis had its refinement but Egypt held onto its primitive, barbaric ways, and from that difference, two very different worlds were born—the one that sprang from the remnants of the great mother culture, and the one that chose a far different path—a path of eventual patriarchal command.

The knowledge of Atlantis was taken in by Egypt but what it did with it was a representation of its yang aspects. The great mother culture that permeated earlier Atlantis had broken down, but still its later representations would eventually find their way into the areas of the world you now know as Scandinavia, the United Kingdom, and Europe.

The manifestation in the Americas is a far different story, and for another time.

Atlantis reached and held its pinnacle point far longer than Egypt. It was a place that moved in and out of form, so in that sense, there was more freedom to shift between physicality and spirit. Much was learned by experiencing those transitory states of being. And more memory was retained by so doing. When the power plants were corrupted with the darker forces of celestial command, things began to go awry. And there seemed a need to begin to repress the teachings that were given to all Atlanteans as their birthright, especially in the use of power in and out of form.

In ancient Egypt, the power of the feminine ways gave way to the insatiable needs and desires of men whom lusted for power, both political and sexual. The magic from Atlantis had been reduced by a priesthood seeking domination over society and seeking to control by ritual magic of unseen forces – forces that did not have the needs of the people in mind.

For whatever reasons, and there are many, my beloved Egypt, in all its splendor and sophistication in the royal courts, was inherently flawed by its deep tie to visceral and sensual sexuality. It wasn't a sexuality rooted in the earth wisdom, but rather in the desires of lust and control that sprang from the bondage of sexual pleasures, rituals that captured female sexual energy and used it for their own gain. And so the teachings had to be veiled by certain temples that were not corrupted, so that it could remain safe and out of the hands of those who wished to utilize its vast power in ways that will go unmentioned.

Both cultures were using principles of magic to define their experience. Atlantis was using these principles more mathematically and scientifically, but not in the way your Western mind will imagine. It was the consciousness of harmonic proportion.

Egypt used this system, and in the beginning, there was great excitement for the endless possibilities that were born of this ideal knowledge. But, given the ebb and flow of the celestial cycles, Egypt was destined to fall deeper into their physical bodies. What they were not prepared for was the density to which so many souls would be trapped. And the feelings were, in a way, so new to the human experience, that the power of those feelings was also destined to seduce a civilization into slavery of the ego. The teachings that were given to the Atlanteans as their birthright became the privilege of just a few in Egypt, as time went on.

To say that power and might were expressed in Egypt is true; it's just that this power and might moved in a direction that became its demise. And yet there was such a raw and intense beauty in the land of Khem that was like no other. It was seductive and sensual and primitive and it was sophisticated and intelligent and held a great respect for the movement of the stars.

With all its complexities and contradictions, Egypt was like no other place on earth!

Were the codes that are carried in the blood immediately released after initiation?

The awareness carried in the bloodstream and the cells of our body do not immediately respond to initiation. We must first clear layers of programming within our cellular structure. The purpose of initiations is to move through a series of coded steps of releasing the memories that reside within all of us. We have needed to do the inner work of transfiguration for a very, very long time. Eventually that will change but for now, the process of initiation serves to align our frequency with that of the cosmic sounds, and of course, the cosmic light.

Once that happens, the full Records of All can be experienced. And even those records have layers of perception embedded within their frequency. The age-old Master Thoth Tehuti had something to do with that – with the system of how we connect to that library of information.

Were there other people around you who were in the know, who were helping to prepare you for your mission?

Yes.

There have always been those who have gone before that assist the next generation with the process of alighting the light field, or light body, around the human physical body. The ancestors all entrain their light with the light of the Shining Ones.

What does this new cycle of time, post December 21, 2012, have in store for us?

This new cycle of time is an about-face. The old structures will redefine themselves with the energies of sustainability through right action. If not, they will fall, including the human power structure that is the oldest one known to you – the Vatican.

There is an older one that is and has always been aligned to the light. They are active in your world even to this day, and they assist your transition in many ways. But they remain unnamed for now because it is not time yet to understand their purpose. More choices must be made by you as a species before you will gain access to these teachings, for contained in them is great cosmic power.

So, we tell you – release the past and remove your resistance to all things supported by truth and love and wisdom and right action. Make your choices wisely and let go of all expectations. If you allow love and forgiveness to move within you, you will discover a light that surpasses anything you have ever experienced here on earth.

Your planet is facing the center of the galaxy unencumbered by your past states of being. If you embrace new thought-forms that are part of the galactic light wave pulsating toward earth, you will find it easier to make this adjustment.

This light wave will get stronger. It will appear as if so many are losing their minds or just leaving their bodies or both. You must understand that this is a process of natural selection, from a viewpoint of frequency and vibration. This light oscillates faster and many are being affected by its rapid rate. This makes the new cycle scary to many as their fear is driving their behavior. I do not wish to judge this response but rather explain the nature of the chaos at this time so that those who choose to be here can come into relationship with divine proportion and learn how to use it wisely. It is immensely powerful. It is a gift of this new cycle of time, and I bet you're not hearing about that on the evening news!

Were your children initiated into the Mysteries?

Yes, they were initiated into the Mysteries. Truly I tell you their initiations began long before their physical birth!

There was a practice our community engaged in that helped purify thoughts and dreams, so that only the most selected windows of opportunity opened for those organizing patterns of thought-forms to enter into our dreaming life. It was an ancient practice of allowing certain codes from the sun to enter into our bloodstream at selected times. So, the babies were born with that awareness and pattern already activated in their DNA.

If so, how many generations were subsequently initiated into the mysteries?

All generations from our time to the present day have been initiated into the Mysteries.

Some generations were able to accomplish more than others, and there are different reasons for that. For some it was timing, and I mean a profound knowledge of celestial timing.

For others it was a lack of interest. Pursuing this knowledge meant responsibilities they were not willing to take on. Many royal houses fell into disrepair and succumbed to the ego. They ignored the Mysteries. This caused great tension among the conglomerate of families because their manifesto required perpetual ascendancy.

As outrageous as the statement I am about to make may sound to you, it is true. Sad but true. Some of the worst offenders of your medieval times, those who persecuted our people, were individuals who were so tired of the responsibilities and burdens of the guardianship of the grail.

They were so angry and so traumatized by their past incarnations where they chose to protect the grail that they came back to destroy it!

In their minds, that was the only way to stop the persecution. But in their polarized states, they created more of what they did not want.

What was life like in your time?

Life in our time was very hard. We were an occupied people, and death was everywhere. There was cruelty and hardship and extreme loss of memory. But even with these extreme and dire circumstances, we managed to laugh and sing and pray to our Maker.

We danced the sacred dances. The sacred dancing by the fire was one of my favorite things. I loved to dance with Yeshua. He was a great dancer. He would dance until he merged with the flames and became a tower of burning light. In this way he connected all of us to the natural elements, to the land, and to each other. And in that connection great trust was born.

The original language of our people held great power and we wished for it to be so, for we were in accordance with the primal sounds that came upon the earth during Creation. We knew them and understood their inborn structure. And in that knowing, we became more fully alive.

Contrast that incredible life force with a majority population who, stripped of their memories, were like the walking dead. We wished for everyone to be free and more fully alive, but that was not to be in my time.

The struggles of my people were difficult to watch. Despite that, I rose to the sun every morning and strengthened myself each day, for that prepared me for the rigors of life at that time.

How is it the same as now, and different from now?

People struggled with family and friends and relationships, just as they do now.

But there was far less awareness outside our community and because of this, you had to be careful when you traveled from place to place. People were more barbaric and violent, and they overreacted to situations. They lost their memories and with it, their ability to discern right action in the moment. A very dangerous and heightened situation could arise out of nowhere.

Now, despite what is being reported in your media, there are a great number of kinder, gentler people in the world. There is a growing consensus of awakening and it is wonderful to see. There are so many random and deliberate acts of kindness. And these acts are infusing light into your world at this time in ways you cannot imagine!

But the same barbaric nature that was in the mind of man still prevails in man.

That is why such weapons of global destruction were conceived and developed. And until more of you realize the scope of these atrocities, and decide against warfare as an acceptable solution to the problems of the Fallen Memories, this evil will still walk the earth. This is the problem that has not been addressed – it is in your MINDS that evil lurks.

You must wipe it clean from your Memories Database. As you go deeper into this cycle of time, you will get better at this. But right now, you stand on a very dangerous precipice. Yes, there are more truth-seekers than ever before on the planet. And that is because you are all needed, each and every one of you, to make the right decisions at the right time, and birth more light within and all around you. That is how you will change the world – biochemically, physiologically, mentally, materially, spiritually, emotionally.

There are many more people in your world who are kinder and gentler and have reclaimed their memories. They are needed because the dangers you face in people who have gone off the deep end, while not prevalent in numbers, are far bigger than in our time. We did not have the means to destroy the earth back then. The difference now is that your leaders and those who wish to bring harm and pain and suffering to others, possess the wealth and ability to destroy your planet.

But no matter how powerful those forces believe themselves to be, that option will not be allowed to come to fruition. Mankind will once again be removed from the earth if it is necessary, save a few, and civilization will reboot itself. That has been and will continue to be the cosmic edict!

You have mentioned "right action" a few times. How do we take "right action"?

You must break free from the bondage to ego. And by that I mean, you must see the bigger picture of your experience. You must realize that old patterned responses will lead to old outcomes. And you are so tired of these outcomes. You are so weary of the hurt and betrayal and suffering they have caused you as a people.

But if you are in bondage to the ego, then you are stuck in patterns of behavior that lead nowhere. Bondage is a terrible state of mind and results in addiction, in one form or another. It is a state of extreme fixation and limitation.

The impulse of the new cycle of time is all about freedom. That's why the battleground for this impulse is being waged in America. It is there where the freedom impulse thrives, and it is directly under attack at this time.

❖ ❖ ❖

As I said before, you have arrived at the place of reconciliation. And as you begin your rise after all these cycles of time, you will ascend by nurturing the inner light. It is the key to your renewal. But in order to do so, slavery to the ego must be abolished. It is what keeps you in conflict with your true nature. It keeps you out of balance. It keeps you in a polarized state of being. And in that state, you are weakened. Those in control understand your desire to break free. But they know it can be restrained by fear, especially fear of losing your material belongings. It is a hideous game that is being played out! Again I say, the way to shift from the fear embedded in your mind is to end the debate with ego.

As that is accomplished, life unfolds endlessly. You live your bigger story. And when you remember the power within you as a sacred skill born from the Creator, you begin to gather all your memories. And those memories lead directly to the heart.

When the heart leads your choices, its vast intelligence can reveal new pathways. Right action becomes your navigational compass. It moves within you and all around you and allows for choices that spring forth from love and trust and the wisdom teachings that are encoded inside your cellular make-up. Yes, all the answers are truly within you!

When the heart center is opened and thriving, the cosmic blueprint becomes activated. Your fuller self emerges and guides you daily as you strive to live your destiny, whatever that may be.

Heart-inspired living must lead the way out of this mess now. It is the only way through the eye of the needle. That is what we are passing through right now. The only way through the eye of the needle is to thread it with right action.

Right action mends the tear in the fabric of the space-time continuum.

It allows for the restoration of your world and all that is in it. That alone should inspire you to right action, but if it does not, consider this. Right action is contagious.

Demand your leaders to be beacons of right action. Demand it and you will see a shift to state of affairs of right action unfolding before your very eyes.

✤ ✤ ✤

For better or for worse, what influence is modern technology having on us at this time?

What you haven't figured out is that your technology is a reflection of your consciousness. All that you can do now because of technology makes your world smarter and more informed, more efficient. It gets the word out to so many people so quickly. Realize how fast the speed of your thoughts can travel across time. It is a marvel to watch what your civilization is now creating for the benefit of mankind. But it comes at a price.

The irony of all this connected energy is that you are disconnected in other ways. You are riding a flow but that flow is not rooted. There is recognition on a global scale but so many people fail to recognize the needs of those closest to them, including themselves.

Yeshua and I do believe this is changing but we emphasize that while connected energy to millions can spread a thought in an instant, you must pay attention to those around you and help them in their struggles to reach for the light. For the more of you that come to the light together, the more you will illuminate not just this world, but your universe.

Were more people open minded to the Mystery Schools in your time?

You have to understand that the general population was uneducated and illiterate at that time. They could not read nor write. Many of these people were born into slavery of some kind.

In the very ancient days, way before my time on earth in a physical body, there was a far greater awareness and the Mystery Schools were not needed. Everyone and everything was a living, conscious being. There were dangers because everything was so alive, and this included the instantaneous manifestation of primal thought, or that fear before something is born.

People used the power of the mind and their emotions to navigate the universe. They used their innate powers to create all of their experiences. Sometimes these experiences would manifest a situation that would kill them, but they could come back into form quickly and try something different. So attachment to ego was not yet developed within the mind.

These were in the days of Zep Tepi. The creational beings were everywhere. They were experimenting with all kinds of genetic material to influence evolution on all levels.

The Mystery Schools came later when we fell deeper into separation from our connection to our Maker. There was a separation between those who understood the most ancient of ways, and those who had simply forgotten. It was as if they fell into amnesia and could not remember their inner powers. The ruling class took advantage of this and pushed them into slavery, creating such harsh conditions and making the need to survive so prevalent that most times it was all most people could think about. It was the primal thought used against its own mind, harnessed into slavery of the ego thought sphere. And believe me, when you are starving and cold, beaten and broken, your mind will do things you cannot imagine. History is full of these examples of desperation.

And yet, the light survived. The sacred fires have never gone out.

There were many people who kept the Mysteries alive from generation to generation. And they did so at great risk to their life.

How do we learn what you learned? How do we do what you did?

Learning and doing are two very different aspects of enlightenment.

Learning requires devotion, discipline, and study and a sincere desire to move beyond your understanding of mundane reality and into the world of magic and phenomenon. And I say magic not in the sense of a magician or sorcerer but High Magic derived from rule and number, from voice and canister, from the golden mean of proportion.

This High Magic involves the use of sound, especially primordial sound, to open doorways into other dimensions. These doorways are within the space around you. And they are inside of you as well. Once opened, other world phenomena take shape right before your very eyes.

Learning is becoming aware of the sensory perceptions that permeate your reality and distinguishing the subtleties of these perceptions.

Doing is putting into practice what you are learning.

In this way you will see reflected back to you where you are with your soul's development. You will learn that you must clear the emotional and mental body of all friction that is past and not relevant to your present experience. Resistance is a charge that puts up a wall between where you are and where you want to be, how you want to be. It is the tension that stalls your movement.

Clearing your emotional body can be the most difficult thing you will do while embodied on earth because it contains all your beliefs and patterning. There is physical pain associated with clearing these beliefs and patterning. There are eons of attachment to these beliefs and patterning. So please hear what I say. You can care about people and places and things but to "attach" to them is to create unnecessary bondage of the soul to the physical. And the key word here is BONDAGE.

You will be challenged in your initiations to sever the cords of bondage to the ego through karmic completion, emotional detachment, and purification. It is an age-old process.

That's why the temples along the Nile were set up the way they were – to allow initiates to learn their lessons and move on, eliminating limiting belief systems and expanding consciousness in the process. When you *experience* your thoughts, that sensation opens a door for a biological release of emotion to move through you. It is alchemy at its finest!

Once you clear yourself from memories held deep in your unconscious mind, and let go of mental limitation, you will begin to experience synchronicity perpetually unfolding. That continuum is very alive and active, but often ignored. Yes it requires courage to walk through the door of that unknown. But once you surrender to the impulse of the primal fear of the unknown before birth, you will find a world of living color, of sight and sound, touch and taste, and aroma that exceeds your imagination. A shining spectrum of rainbows is released within the bloodstream and you then open like the peacock's tail.

It is the Gate of the Eleven, and it is what Yeshua and I opened together.

But before that, both Yeshua and I had to undergo our initiations separately and then together. So this is what I did – in the temples, on the land, and within myself. It was my destiny to transform myself in this way. I took my studies very seriously and was completely and utterly devoted to them. Sometimes Yeshua would tease me about my seriousness and then start laughing at me. That infectious laugh of his could dispel my frustration, and make the sun shine on my darkest of days. He had such a soothing effect on me at times when I needed to truly lighten up.

As I have said before, my mother recognized my devotion from a very young age and never wavered in her belief in me. Even when I clearly disappointed her expectations, she was right by my side, encouraging me to press on. She would hold me tight and whisper in my ear – "Miriam, you are a child of God. All is possible. Believe in yourself."

Can anyone learn the Mysteries?

Anyone can learn the mysteries, but will they?

You must have a will and determination, and your heart must be purified along the way. That is the grail path. But the Mysteries are available to each and every one of you as your birthright here on earth. Never forget that!

Yet you must be ready to ride rushing rivers of emotions embedded in your psyche, cross bridges into the most-dreaded unknown, climb jagged mountains that rise up from within you, and sail the vast oceans of the Memory of All. If you are willing to do that and more, the Mysteries will be revealed unto you.

Do you need special gifts to learn the Mysteries?

You don't need special gifts to learn the mysteries but you need a special desire to do so. You must focus on your strengths. You must free your gifts of spirit so that they can work for you, rather than hold onto restrictive behavior that only seeks to hold you back.

Everyone has gifts. But not everyone sees their gifts.

For those that see their gifts, not everyone uses them. And for those that use them, not everyone uses their full potential.

So you can begin to see how all these choices lead your way.

Make your choices and allow them to create your experiences. Let these experiences reflect back to you what you need to learn to move beyond limitation, beyond the horizon and into the Gate of the Eleven.

I will not go into detail on how the Gate of the Eleven works at this time but I will say this. When you reach that gate, all parts of you from all dimensional realities come together into one, and you receive your full cosmic potential. That is what the life of Yeshua was truly about.

Remember you are always creating your reality, whether consciously or not. You are always participating in your reality, whether consciously or not. It is all your choice.

So if you want to learn what I learned and do what I did, this is the way in which it was done. This is the process in general terms. It requires a passion for the truth, it requires a heart that knows love and forgiveness, and it requires a determination to go the distance. Sometimes you don't start out with all these attributes in place. You learn by your initiations and pick up these qualities along the way. But you must have a burning desire to experience the light beyond the darkness.

Once you are free from the charge the mirror images present you, the seals are broken and more fluid states of being are opened for you to experience. You are still navigating in the physical realm on earth, but you have more dimensions with which to experience that realm.

There are pockets of magic sewn in all over the fabric of space time and when you are traveling lightly, you are able to jump in and out of them, according to your desires.

Believe in yourself, steer the course to your destiny and all will come to you in time. Trust the timing of what you learn and what you do. That timing is a sequence of events that tests your readiness to vibrate differently in space and time.

And remember – the Gate of the Eleven awaits you!

VESICA PISCES

Chapter 5

VESICA PISCES:
THE LESSON OF HER GEMATRIA

In order to understand the gematria of Mary Magdalene, we must first understand gematria.

Author and teacher Gregg Braden talks about it on his CD called *The God Code*. He says that modern science describes our world as words, elements, and numbers, and that ancient traditions employed the same practice. "One of the secrets of ancient languages...was to describe the secret that every alphabet that's ever been recorded has always had hidden or secret numbers connected to every letter of the alphabet." Braden goes on to say the numbers are precise, specific, and very mysterious. He adds that "this ancient science and it is a science, of applying numbers to find the deeper meaning in the texts" has a name. It's called gematria, and is similar to numerology.

Gematria was used to encode sacred texts. It's been in practice since the ancient of days. In it, certain concepts were conveyed by the scribe to the initiate by the use of these numbers. From

American author Margaret Starbird, we learn of Mary Magdalene's number code based on her gematria in the New Testament. In Starbird's book, *Mary Magdalene: Bride in Exile*, she includes a CD which contains a 2005 lecture given by her. In that lecture, she begins by telling us that gematria is used in both Hebrew and Greek. "Both languages have the capacity to be added into phrases and then reflecting numbers of the cosmic principles. In Hebrew, and also in Greek, each letter has a numeric value. So if you named someone a specific name, or gave them a specific title, or even coined a specific phrase, you can carry the energy of the cosmic principle because the way you spell that phrase adds up to a certain number that is already a part of the canon of sacred geometry."

You carry the energy of the cosmic principle in the number ascribed to a name.

All the Mary's in the New Testament – specifically Maria – add up to 152. Starbird gives the numerical breakdown of the alphabet letters on page 155 of her book *The Goddess in the Gospels – Reclaiming the Sacred Feminine*. She tells us that these women named Mary/Maria "are associated with this important feminine principle by virtue of gematria of their shared name Maria, 152. But the epithet of one Mary, the Magdalene…bears the exact sum 153." On page 160 of *Goddess in the Gospels*, she writes out Mary's exact title.

Starbird emphasizes that English author John Michel talked about the importance of the number 153, "and the 153 as the root and matrix of all geometric figures". He correlates 153 to the vesica pisces. John Michel related it to Maria, or Mother Mary. But

Starbird says we must look to the Greek that was in the gospel at the time it was written.

Starbird concludes her examination in simple yet profound words. She says that "all the Mary's in the gospel are holy but only one of them is the Holy of Holies. She nails it with her title. That title didn't come from a town. That title was made for her to tell you who she was. She was the…the Tower of the Flock, and she was the 153, the bride, the vessel…"

Now that's a far cry from being a prostitute! So how did she go from goddess to whore?

That mess came about in the fifth century when Pope Gregory I conflated the fallen woman in the New Testament account with that of Mary Magdalene. Just because he was pope and just because he said it, it was accepted as truth from that point on. End of story.

In *The Complete Idiot's Guide to Mary Magdalene*, Lesa Bellevie writes on page 27 that during his reign, there was much confusion about who Mary Magdalene was. "During his reign, Pope Gregory delivered a homily in which he said: 'She whom Luke calls the sinful woman, whom John calls Mary, we believe to be the Mary from whom seven devils were ejected according to Mark.' "

"Gregory made the decision to reduce confusion and to unify church doctrine. His decision, to conflate Mary Magdalene, Mary of Bethany, and Luke's sinner, may not have been the *best* decision, but it was by no means an innovation. What he *was* responsible for was ending any real discussion of Mary Magdalene's true identity."

For about 1,400 years, Gregory's declaration was, officially, the end of the story." [*The Complete Idiot's Guide to Mary Magdalene*, p. 27]

We have the ancient writers ascribing numbers according to her title and referring to Mary Magdalene as the goddess. Then we have the denigration of her status to a prostitute by Pope Gregory I. And unfortunately, this label lasted for so long that even when the papal bull of 1969 officially stated Mary was not a prostitute, it went largely unnoticed!

"In 1969, the Catholic Church removed from the liturgical calendar the appellative of 'penitent' traditionally given to Mary Magdalene; likewise, from that date the lecture from the Gospel of Luke (Lk 7: 36-50) about the sinful woman ceased to be used in the liturgy of the Feast of Mary Magdalene. Since then, the Catholic Church has no longer considered Mary Magdalene a repentant prostitute. However, this remains the prevailing view for many Catholics." This quote can be found at http://www.vopus. org/en/gnosis/alchemy/mary-magdalene.html.

Right around the time that papal bull was issued, *Jesus Christ Superstar* was a smash hit on Broadway. The rock opera was my favorite musical. But regrettably it cast Mary Magdalene in the same old light as a prostitute. With all the social change afoot at that time, it's hard to believe we still didn't get her story straight.

What does that tell me about the lesson of her gematria?

For one thing, it tells me that numbers cannot be corrupted. Numbers are what they are, and when they're used to further describe words, pay attention. The words of texts can be corrupted for a variety of reasons, but numbers tell the story. The games of the gods are hidden in the numbers!

Another thing I see so clearly now is how past history was written by those in power. You had to know how to write, or make someone who could write, record the version you wanted chronicled at the time. Much of our past history is simply not objective.

Many people today, especially in America, don't realize what a stranglehold the Holy Roman Catholic Church had on every aspect of people's lives for a very, very long time. As the hierarchy of the church – which was derived from tenets of the Roman Empire – forcefully eliminated paganism in all forms, they cruelly and sadistically crushed alternate belief systems and censored many books from the traditional bible along the way. The variety of existing information was sacrificed for a few.

Thankfully, perhaps through divine intervention, the incredible finds of alternate "biblical" texts at Nag Hammadi, found in Upper Egypt in 1945, and the Dead Sea Scrolls found at Qumran on the shores of the Dead Sea between 1947-1956, we now have other books from which to draw knowledge and insights regarding the biblical stories. From the Nag Hammadi texts come books like The Gospel of Thomas, The Gospel of Mary, and The Gospel of Truth, to name a few. And from the Dead Sea Scrolls found in a desert cave in 1952 came an intriguing text called the Copper Scroll, which is a list of buried treasure. Yes, buried treasure!

With these additional texts, we can now expand the possibilities of the Jesus story, and other stories as well. We can learn fascinating details, like the difficulty that Mary Magdalene had as a woman, she the Master of the Mysteries, she whom Jesus loved.

If the lesson of her gematria has taught me anything in my search to uncover the hidden truth, it taught me that the truth of who she was…was hidden in plain sight all along. All I had to do was look at the numbers. The numbers don't lie.

It has taken me years to figure these things out, to put these pieces together, and shake off the brainwashing that was part of my religious upbringing. I don't fault my parents; they simply taught me what they were taught. And they were taught not to question the authority of the church.

I credit my father for giving my brother and me the choice to pick our schools, once he retired from the military and we entered civilian life as a family. My mother wanted us to go to Catholic schools, but he overrode my mother's wishes and gave us a choice. If we chose public schools, he said we would have to continue our religious education in catechism, which was held after school. And we would still have to go to confession and church every week.

Yet even with those restrictions, it was a no-brainer for my brother and me. We chose public schools and never looked back. By the time I was a teenager, I began to question the church's teachings so strongly that my parents finally relented and said I didn't have to go to church anymore. I was thrilled but it wasn't because I didn't believe in god or Jesus, but rather I didn't believe in the church's teachings. And even though it took me many years to pass through the gates of shame and guilt, I finally set out on my own unique journey to understand the true Jesus story, which eventually opened the door to the true story of Mary Magdalene.

My lesson has been to learn to question everything. This simple principle was taught to me so eloquently on my trips to Rennes le Chateau, France. Henry vigorously maintained that everything must be examined and questioned. Go back to square one and start over as many times as necessary to get things right, he would remind me.

I can say with absolute conviction that, once I began to question everything, the truth that revealed itself was far more interesting than old stories handed down, stripped of their true meaning.

At this time in our history we must be brave enough and diligent enough to do the spiritual work of inner transformation. We must stop our self-destructive nonsense and face the truth of our behavior. We can either be in flow with the cosmic energies of change or we can be in resistance to them. But either way, change is upon us.

The lesson of her gematria is that Mary Magdalene was a woman of power who was also a great teacher. She overcame the obstacles of her time and continued her teachings, passing down the knowledge of the Mysteries to those who would swear to keep the teachings sacred and secret until the time of the great awakening. And that time is now.

That this most beautiful and intelligent soul we know as Mary Magdalene is emerging for so many at this time, is no surprise to me. From a karmic perspective, it makes perfect sense.

The Dalai Lama said in September 2009 at the Vancouver Peace Summit that western women would change our world. His exact words were "the world will be saved by the Western woman." Now why do you think he said that? What could have motivated him to say such a thing?

The Dalai Lama is a wise man. And from his mouth comes the clarion call for those of us who are privileged enough and passionate enough to live in a society that promotes our freedom, our right to speak up, and our right to demand change in this world.

The gematria of Mary's name tells me some things just cannot be corrupted and that truth will find its way to the surface in the fullness of time.

It also reflects back to me my disappointment, despair, and deep disillusionment with the old ways of the world in the very dark times. These times were full of distortions perpetrated on us by others, others who either didn't know her status, or had an agenda that did not serve the truth of her identity. Her abilities were crushed under the mantle of suffering and penance.

Yet the gematria of her name informs me of the high regard for Mary Magdalene while she walked the earth. She was an avatar; she embodied the goddess.

The indigenous people worldwide understand our evolution is deeply connected to the rhythms and vibrations of the marriage of heaven and earth. In this sacred eternal dance of the bride and the bridegroom, we are given an opportunity to rise above where we have been, and step into a brave new world that is alive and pulsing with the heartbeat of the great earth in union with the cosmic forces. It is alignment at its best, and it affords us the chance to experience harmony with ourselves and with others, once we stop creating our reality from a dualistic mind.

It is a moment in time for us to truly see ourselves in all our glorious potential, and in this quest, the gracious and impeccable spirit of Mary Magdalene is leading the way. She has always told me that love and forgiveness open the door to the Mysteries, and I have found that to be true.

The lesson of her gematria is that her greatness was always there, waiting to be rediscovered by those who would take the time to question, for those who would take the time to care, for those who would forgive, and for those who would love with an open heart, no matter what.

As her most gracious spirit appears to so many of us at this time of the transition of the ages, may she inspire us to seek the truth of her story and of her teachings. May she reflect the possibility that the evolution of her story is the evolution of our own...

Acknowledgments

I would like to thank Rene Barnett for suggesting to me to write this book. It came about in one of our many telephone conversations between East Coast and West Coast. She told me when she read the passages in my novels attributed to Mary Magdalene, that she really felt something unique was going on. She felt she was hearing Mary's voice. And that inspired me.

I would also like to thank Betsy Ritchie and Kim Bacik for submitting questions to Mary. Their curiosity gave me motivation, especially Kim's awe of Mary's revelations.

Thanks to Mark Zarrillo for designing the lovely original cover. And thanks to Matthew Giorgio for the exquisite redesign.

Thanks to Brian Kannard of Grave Distractions Publications for his enduring professional assistance and support of my books from the very beginning.

And lastly, to all of you who have gathered in The Magdalene Circles all these years, and for those that have passed through from time to time. To all of you who have read my books and excitedly wait for the next one, and for all that have shown up to events I have hosted in her name.

You have heard the voice of the Magdalene. You have witnessed the healing power of her incredible spirit. You have taken the time to smell the roses that spring from her garden. You have tasted the waters that run through her lands, she the first century avatar who creates the magic...

About the Author

Gloria Amendola is an intuitive who has a passion for esoteric knowledge and dream language. In her private circles, she blends the western tradition of research and evidence with the eastern path of meditation and going within for answers. She is a trained facilitator and accomplished shamanic drummer, and works with a variety of disciplines in her teaching.

Her travels bring her to sacred sites worldwide to experience these powerful landscape temples firsthand. A modern-day Templar aligned to Rennes le Chateau, France, she follows in the footsteps of the enigmatic Knights Templar, walking where they walked, gathering impressions from the traces they left behind.

Mary Magdalene: Revelations From A First Century Avatar is Gloria's first hybrid non-fiction/ channeled book.

Other titles include her novels in the *Tower* series. They are *"The Tower and the Dream—Awakening to the Call,"* and *"The Tower and the Land—Awakening to the Light."*